music for Memorial & Thanksgiving Services for manuals

EDITED & ARRANGED BY

C. H. TREVOR

NOVELLO PUBLISHING LIMITED
8/9 Frith Street, London W1V 5TZ

Order No: NOV 262778

EDITORIAL NOTE

Although the pieces in this book have suggestions for registration on an organ of two (and sometimes three) manuals, they can be played effectively on a one-manual instrument with appropriate stops. The pedals can be used at the player's discretion. When the dynamics only are given, the choice of registration is left to the player.

As stops with the same names do not always produce the same effect on different organs, other registrations should be used if those suggested are not effective or suitable on any particular instrument. The directions for registration in brackets may be used or not at the player's discretion.

If the organ is an unenclosed one-manual, the dynamics should be ignored except where it is possible to change the registration without interrupting the flow of the music.

Most of the pieces in this book are suitable for use on other occasions.

Certain sections and repeats may be omitted if a piece is found to be too long for the required time.

C.H.T.

CONTENTS

		Page
Nimrod from *Variations Op. 36*	ELGAR	2
March from *Idomeneo*	MOZART	3
Offertoire	DANDRIEU	4
March	PURCELL	6
Minuet	PURCELL	6
Gavotte from *Orchestral Suite No. 3*	J. S. BACH	7
Aria	PARADIES	8
Preludium from *Missa Solemnis*	BEETHOVEN	10
March from *Die Zauberflöte*	MOZART	11
Musette from *Alcina*	HANDEL	12
Two Equali	BEETHOVEN	13
Minuet from *Samson*	HANDEL	14
March from *Occasional Oratorio*	HANDEL	15
Chaconne	L. COUPERIN	16
Prière	FRANCK	18
March from *Scipio*	HANDEL	18
Méditation	BOËLLMANN	19
Trumpet Tune	PURCELL	20

NIMROD

from *Variations Op.36*

Sw. Diapason 8. using Sw. Pedal
or Diapason(s) 8. (4.) or Flutes 8.4. if organ
is an unenclosed one manual.

Elgar

© 1977 by ELKIN & CO. LTD.   E 2778   All Rights Reserved

MARCH
from *Idomeneo*

Gt. Diapason 8.
Sw. Diapason 8.

Mozart

OFFERTOIRE

Gt.
Sw.} Diapason 8.

Jean François Dandrieu
(1684-1740)

Lento

Gt. Diapasons 8. 4.
Sw. Diapasons 8. 4. 2. (box open)
Sw. to Gt.

Allegretto

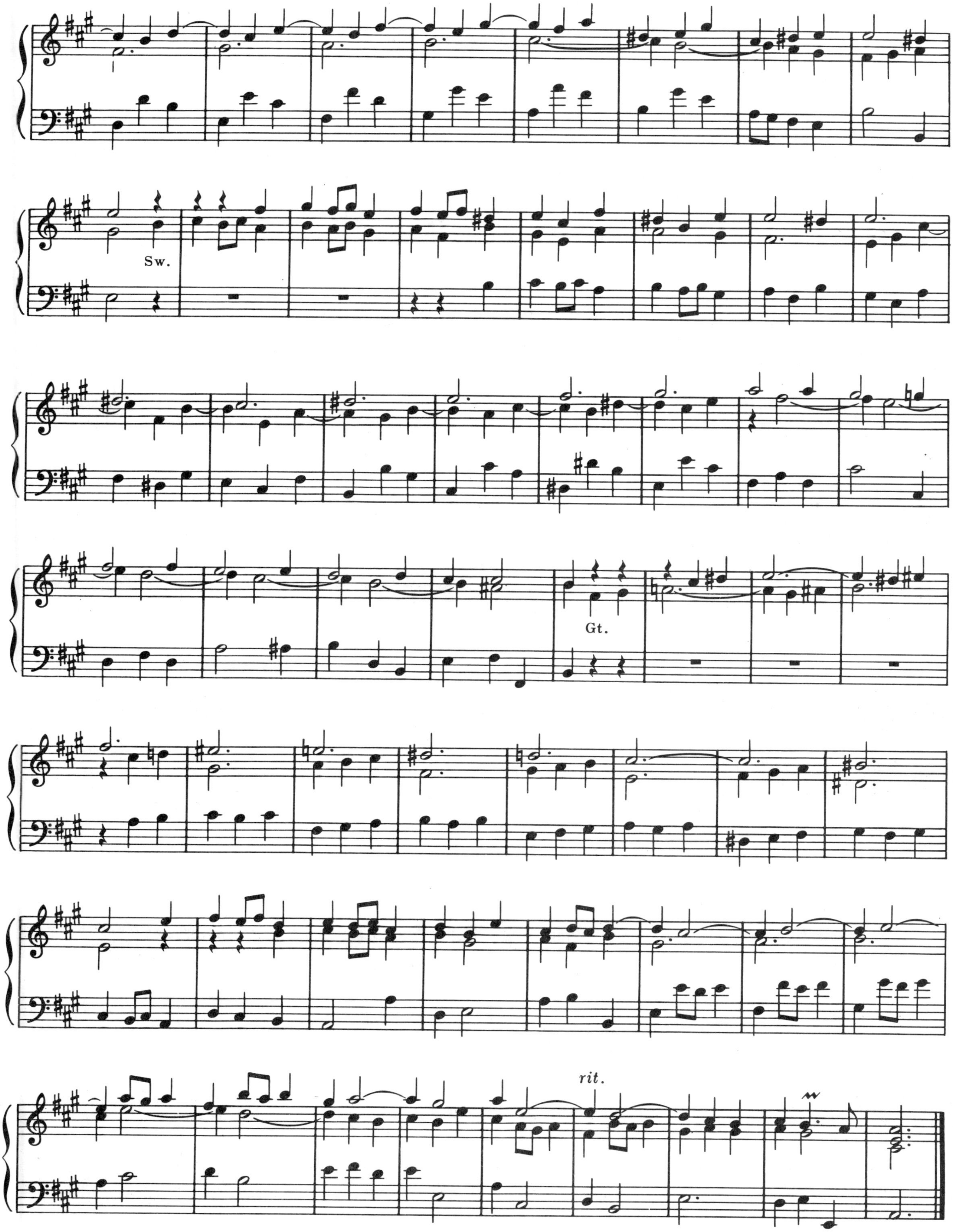
Sw.
Gt.
rit.

MARCH

Gt. light Diapasons 8. 4. (2.)

Moderato

Purcell

MINUET

Flute(s) 8. (4.)

Andante grazioso

Purcell

GAVOTTE
from *Orchestral Suite No. 3*

Gt. 8. 4. (2.)
Sw. 8. 4. (2.)

J. S. Bach

Moderato

If preferred, this piece can be played throughout on Gt. light Diapasons (or Flutes) 8.4.

ARIA

Gt. Flute (or Dulciana) 8.
Sw. soft 8.
Ch. Flutes 8. 4.

Domenico Paradies
(1707-1791)

Larghetto e cantabile

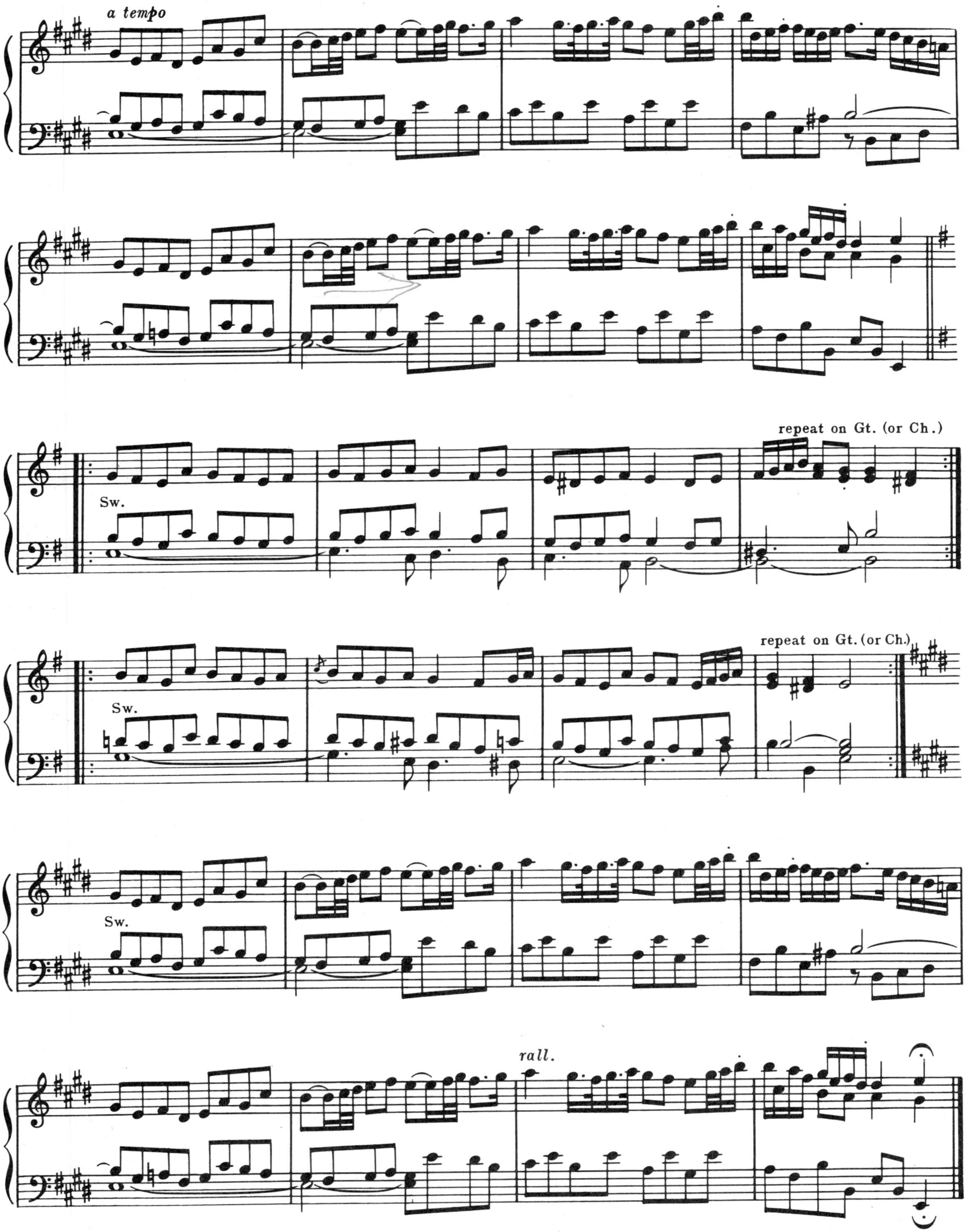
a tempo
Sw.
repeat on Gt. (or Ch.)
Sw.
repeat on Gt. (or Ch.)
Sw.
rall.

PRELUDIUM
from *Missa Solemnis*

Sw. Diapason 8.

Beethoven

Adagio sostenuto

MARCH
from *Die Zauberflöte*

Gt. Diapason(s) 8. (4.)
Sw. Diapason(s) 8. (4.)

Mozart

MUSETTE
from *Alcina*

Gt. (or Ch.) Flute(s) 8. (4.)
[or Sw. Diapason 8.]

Handel

TWO EQUALI
originally written for four trombones

Sw. Oboe (or Diapason) 8. (box closed)

Beethoven

MINUET
from *Samson*

Gt. Flutes 8. 4.
Sw. Diapason 8. (or Flutes 8. 4.)
Sw. to Gt.

Handel

MARCH
from *Occasional Oratorio*

Handel

CHACONNE

Gt. Diapasons 8.4.
Sw. Diapasons 8.4.2. (box open)
Sw. to Gt.

Louis Couperin
(1626-1661)

Maestoso

17

PRIÈRE

César Franck

Gt. } soft 8.
Sw.
Sw. to Gt.

Quasi lento

p Sw.

più f Gt.

pp Sw.

rall.

pp

If preferred, this piece can be played on the Swell throughout.

MARCH
from *Scipio*

Handel

Maestoso

f

2nd time rall.

MÉDITATION

Boëllmann

The dynamics should be realised by using the Swell pedal.

TRUMPET TUNE

R.H. Trumpet 8.
L.H. 8. 4.(2.)

Purcell

Maestoso

marcato

Alternative registration: Gt. Diapasons 8.4.(2.) both hands.